HOW TO BOX

A Guide for Beginners

HOW TO BOX
A Guide for Beginners

Edward R. Ricciuti

Illustrated by Don Madden

Thomas Y. Crowell   New York

Library of Congress Cataloging in Publication Data
Ricciuti, Edward R.
Boxing for beginners.

Summary: An introduction to the sport of boxing,
which teaches the beginning boxer how to prepare his
mind and body and how to box at a very basic level.
1. Boxing—Juvenile literature.   [1. Boxing]
I. Madden, Don, 1927-   ill.   II. Title.
GV1136.R52 1982   796.8'3   81-43311
ISBN 0-690-04180-2   ACCR2
ISBN 0-690-04181-0 (lib. bdg.)

1 2 3 4 5 6 7 8 9 10
First Edition

In memory of Kelvin Anderson, boxer
who died in an air tragedy
while representing his country in Poland

Contents

HOW TO BOX
A Guide for Beginners

Before You Begin

You pace up and down in a locker room behind the grandstand of a sports arena. The crowd seated in the stands roars. The cheers are for two boxers who are nearly finished with their match. You are next in the ring. But for now, you wait.

Every so often you shuffle your feet, dance a bit on your toes, and punch a few times into the air. Your legs feel strong and springy. Your mind is alert. But you admit to yourself that you are nervous, that butterflies are having a grand time in your stomach. No matter.

1

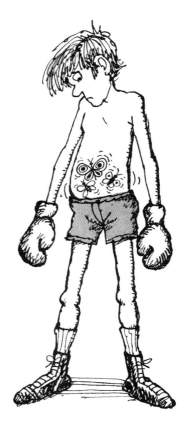

It happens before every match. It's part of the game.

Around you, the smell of perspiration and antiseptic hangs in the air. It is the same in any locker room. As you wait, you smack your boxing gloves into each other. The sound echoes through the room.

Moments later, the door of the locker room opens. A man pokes his head through the opening and calls your name. The other boxers are done. It is your turn. In what seems like hours but really is only seconds, you have walked along an aisle through the seated crowd and climbed up a short wooden staircase leading to the ring. You step through the ropes and go to your corner.

You meet the referee and your opponent. Your second—the man who coaches you in the corner between rounds—slips a rubber mouthpiece into place. Designed to guard your teeth and to prevent them from cutting your lip, the mouthpiece has been soaked in a mixture of water and the same antiseptic you smelled in the locker room.

Then, from ringside, a bell clangs. The match has begun. You forget everything—the crowd, the smells, the butterflies—and enter another world. The only people in it are you and the other boxer. Each of you will begin

3

testing the strength, endurance, reflexes, courage, and skills of the other.

People who do not understand boxing may look upon it as only a brawl—two men swinging wildly at each other, pushing and shoving. A match between two boxers who know their sport, however, is anything but a brawl. Done properly, boxing calls for as much strategy as football, as much grace as tennis, as much dis-

cipline as judo, and as much endurance as long-distance running.

Boxing is as much an art as the other sports, for every move in boxing should accomplish a particular goal—to fool the opponent so he can be hit, for instance, or to tire him. When done right, each punch is a very technical maneuver, the result of mind, feet, legs, arms, and the trunk of the body all working together. A boxer uses a strategy, just like a general does to win a battle. But he does not— or should not—consciously think of each and every move while he boxes. Instead, he should be so well trained that his moves are automatic. He makes them almost without thinking, just like a successful athlete in any sport.

If you already are a boxer all this comes as no surprise. If you are not, and if what you have read so far sounds exciting, you may want to learn more about boxing—perhaps to enjoy it as a spectator or to try it for yourself, to see if it is a sport for you.

This book introduces you to boxing. Here you can find out some basic facts about the sport—what it is and how it is done. You will discover what it takes to be good at boxing. The book will not, however, make you an expert boxer. While it describes many of the tactics and tricks used by boxers, it will not teach you the step-by-step details of how to attack an opponent or defend yourself in the ring. No book can do that. Do not fool yourself into thinking that you can learn how to box well by yourself or even with a friend to help, unless he already is an expert.

The only way to learn how to really box is to do it. That means practice with experienced boxers in a ring under the supervision of knowledgeable boxing coaches. To accomplish this, you must join an organized boxing program. You can find out how to go about this a few pages further on in this book.

What this book *will* do is to get you started. It will teach you exercises to get your body in shape for boxing and some of the most basic boxing techniques. You will learn the right way to stand and move your feet and the best way to throw such punches as the left jab and the straight right. You will learn to drill with a partner, practicing punches by hitting his open glove. By the time you finish this book, if you try the exercises and drills described here, you probably will know whether or not you like boxing well enough to participate regularly in the sport.

AMATEUR BOXING

This book is concerned with amateur boxing—that is, boxing for fun and not money. Professional boxing, boxing for prize money, is another matter altogether.

A professional boxer is a man who earns his living at the sport—or tries to. At the top level of professional boxing, there is much money to be made. Many young boxers enter the sport hoping they can become rich and famous, like Muhammed Ali or Sugar Ray Leonard. Unfortunately, very few make it to the top. Only a handful of professional boxers ever earn enough money to live on for very long or see their dreams of greatness come true. For every Ali or Sugar Ray, there are hundreds of professionals leading lonely, tough lives, training in dirty gyms and boxing for a few dollars in small arenas.

Like most boxers, Sugar Ray and Ali started out as amateurs and remained amateurs for many years. Before either became a professional boxer, he won the highest honor that an amateur can achieve—an Olympic Gold Medal. It takes far more skill to do that than most boxers ever possess. Even so, amateur boxers can find great satisfaction in the ring. All an amateur boxer needs to feel fulfilled is to participate—the reward is in the doing.

There are many levels of amateur boxing,

just as in, say, football there are midget and Pop Warner leagues, then high school and college teams.

There are few if any boxing schools like those at which you pay for lessons—such as judo or karate schools. In fact, a nice part about boxing is that you can learn it free of charge. Most boxing programs are not businesses but are sponsored by clubs and community agencies as a public service. Boxers from these various organizations compete against one another in regular matches. There are boxing tournaments in most parts of the country. The big ones are the Golden Gloves and Junior Olympics. The Junior Olympics are for boys ages 10 through 15 years.

For a long time, Junior Olympic boxing was regulated by the Amateur Athletic Union (AAU), the major nonprofessional sports association in the country outside of intercollegiate sports. Most amateur boxing matches in the United States have been fought under

AAU rules, or at least were until the early 1980s. Then the responsibility changed hands. Now such matches are under the Amateur Boxing Federation, which grew out of the AAU. The rules for boxing have stayed the same, however, and are the safest anywhere in the world.

In recent years, boxing has been mostly a city sport. There were many boxing clubs in urban areas, few in the suburbs or country. Following the success of the United States boxers in the 1976 Olympics, however, amateur boxing gained considerable popularity in this country. Increasingly, boys from the suburbs and country have either headed for boxing clubs in the city to learn the sport or have organized their own clubs. Clubs also have been started in the country. I know of some on farms, in barns.

You may already know of a club in your area. If not, you might find one by contacting the local Catholic Youth Organization, Boys'

Club, or Young Men's Christian Association. Check the police department, too, or your local community center, or recreation department. Or try asking a sportswriter on the staff of the newspaper you read. Watch the sports pages. They may tell of boxing matches sponsored by clubs in your area.

If one of these leads help, write to the AAU in Indianapolis, Indiana. The AAU still handles such requests for the Amateur Boxing Federation. It will put you in touch with a boxing program connected with the federation.

It is important to learn as much as you can about a boxing club before joining it. Make sure the coaches really know the sport and, especially, how to keep it safe. Ask others about the people in charge of the club. Do they have the best interests of the boxers at heart? Have they a reputation for fairness and sportsmanship? Is winning the only thing that matters to them, or are they most concerned about teaching the sport? Your parents or adult friends may be able to help you find the answers. As in other sports organizations, some boxing clubs are better than others. Go with the best.

A Bit about Boxing

BOXING HISTORY

Boxing has been described as the ancient art of hitting with the fists. But long before it was an art, or a sport, it was a means of unarmed combat. No one knows exactly when boxing for sport began. We do know, from carvings, that more than 6,000 years ago, there were boxers in Ancient Egypt. And at least 4,000 years ago, boxing was a part of the training of Greek warriors. In museums today, you can see ancient Greek vases with the figures of boxers painted on them.

The type of boxing carried on by the ancient Greeks was very different from the technical, regulated sport of today. The Greek boxer stood face-to-face with his opponent. With his right hand, he threw wide, looping punches designed to hit the other man in the side of his torso, not straight on in the face and body. He held his left hand near his body to block his opponent's punches. Using brute strength more than skill, the boxers stood toe to toe, hammering away at each other.

Around their fists they wore not gloves but wrappings of leather. Sometimes metal studs were sewed into the wrapping, which was called a "cestus." When the Romans learned

boxing from the Greeks, they made the cestus deadlier by equipping it with spikes.

Boxing became very brutal under the Romans. In fact, boxers usually fought to the death. Because of its terrible nature, boxing disappeared in Rome after the empire became Christianized. During the Dark and

Middle Ages, boxing techniques were mostly forgotten in Europe, although in Asia various forms of hand-to-hand combat using the fists were practiced.

Boxing in the West did not reappear as a sport until about 1719 in England, when a fencing master named James Figg began to teach fighting with bare fists. His style of boxing was based largely on the swordsmanship he knew so well. The boxer was taught to stand like a swordsman, his right side facing his opponent and his right hand held in front of him as if he were gripping a sword. The left arm was kept close to the body as a de-

fense. Today, boxers still use a variation of this position, but with the left hand rather than the right in front.

English boxers fought for prize money—and professional boxing still is called "prize fighting." A match was not broken into rounds separated by rest periods, as is the case today. The boxers simply battled without pause until one man was helpless. They not only punched but pulled hair, gouged eyes, and kicked. And at first they wore no gloves. They fought with bare knuckles.

Before long, however, some basic rules were developed. By the middle of the eighteenth century boxers were given a thirty-second rest after a knockdown. They were not permitted to hit an opponent after he went down. Referees were assigned to make sure the rules were obeyed. And in practice sessions, at least, boxers began to wear padded gloves.

During the first half of the nineteenth century, more rules gradually evolved. Rounds were established but they still ended only when a boxer went down. A square ring surrounded by ropes became the standard arena for boxers. Gouging, butting, kicking, hitting below the belt, and other roughhouse tactics were banned.

Even so, boxing was a far cry from what it is today. Matches often lasted for hours. Bare fists were still the rule in actual bouts. Boxers of any size—big or small—were matched against each other.

Then in about the middle of the century a new set of boxing rules was devised in England. They were the work of a nobleman, John S. Douglas, the Marquis of Queensberry, an avid supporter of boxing. It took several years for his rules to become popular, but by the beginning of the twentieth century they were in force virtually everywhere, and they are the basis for modern boxing.

The Queensberry rules called for three-minute rounds and gloves instead of bare fists. If a boxer went down for a ten-second count, the other man was declared the winner. Weight classes matching men of equal size were established. Boxing no longer looked like a brawl but a smooth, artistic sport.

BOXING INJURIES

Just as bare-fisted boxing was brutal, so in some ways is professional boxing today, although it is much safer than it was in the past. But amateur boxing is something else again. It may surprise you to know that amateur boxing can be among the safest of sports, if carried out under strict rules, like those of the Amateur Boxing Federation. The amateur rules do not allow experienced boxers to go against newcomers to the sport. Boxers are also matched by age groups. Equipment is carefully checked to make sure it meets safety requirements. And matches are stopped if it appears that one boxer is not able to defend himself well enough to avoid even the possibility of a serious injury.

During 1979 and 1980, M. P. Demos, a medical doctor from Miami, Florida, carried out a study of boxing injuries in matches approved by the AAU. Dr. Demos was chairman of Florida's Junior Olympics Boxing and of the Amateur Boxing Federation's Sports Medicine Committee.

Here is some of what Dr. Demos found:

In 6,050 matches, in which a total of 12,100 boxers competed, there were only 174 injuries. Less than two of every 100 boxers were injured—and under injuries Dr. Demos included minor ones, such as bruises, cut lips, and black eyes. Of all the boxers, 103 were seriously harmed. There were two broken jaws, for instance, seven broken thumbs, and two broken arms.

Records from other sports examined by Dr. Demos told a different story. One study of football showed that 81 out of every 100 players suffered an injury. Soccer and basketball had an injury rate of 30 per 100 players. Even tennis had more injuries than boxing. All in all, the average number of players injured for 19 sports other than amateur boxing was 39 out of 100.

One reason for the low injury rate, besides the tough safety rules, is that amateur boxing is a game of skill. Light punches skillfully delivered score as many points as heavy ones.

In other words, it is not so much the damage you do with your fists but how well you use them that is important.

A CONTACT SPORT

This is not to say amateur boxing is not a tough contact sport. Make no mistake about it, boxing is exactly that. Once in a great while—nine times in the 6,050 matches studied by Dr. Demos—a boxer is knocked out, losing his bout. (Knockouts are as rare as they are in amateur boxing because the referee usually stops the match if he sees one boxer getting too much the worst of it. The other is declared the winner.)

Before you begin boxing, think about this: although injuries seldom occur in properly supervised matches, you still pile up points by hitting your opponent with your fists. If that idea does not appeal to you, perhaps boxing is not your kind of sport. Don't be ashamed about it. Not liking to box because you don't want to hit someone does not mean that you lack courage.

If you decide you would like to give it a try, talk to your parents about it. You should get their permission before you start to box.

BOXING, NOT FIGHTING

A boxing coach I know operates a gym in a big-city neighborhood where it is hard to grow up without having to fight on the street. Long before they enter the ring, many of the boys he teaches know too well how to hit, and what it is like to be hit. My friend explains the difference between boxing and fighting this way: "I train my boys to box, to keep their tempers and use their heads, so they don't street fight. They already know how to do that."

25

How would you guys like to turn that dumb stuff you're doing into a sport?
BIG CITY BOXING CLUB

For boys everywhere boxing is a way of being active and proving oneself physically. A boy who becomes a proficient boxer usually knows he can take care of himself in a tight spot. Outside the ring, he doesn't have to fight to prove it.

Boxing is not only a matter of having a strong body and knowing how to get the most out of your muscles, or how to use your fists. Boxing tunes up and toughens the mind. It takes lots of self-discipline to carry on the regular exercise that boxing demands and to concentrate on the details you need for even basic boxing. As you learn to box, do not be surprised if your confidence in what you can accomplish is growing like your muscles. You may learn to do things with your body you might not have thought possible. And like a runner, you may develop not only the physical stamina but also the "heart" to go that extra mile—in a boxer's case, the last, tiring minute of a hard-fought round.

Learning to box as a teenager made me feel better about myself than I ever had before. Some people do not need boxing for this purpose. I did, and the experience has helped me ever since then. There is nothing like winning in the boxing ring—where you are totally on your own without help from any teammate—to make you feel you can win outside the ring as well. I know for sure that I have reached certain goals in life only because of the confidence boxing instilled in me.

Another great benefit of boxing, perhaps best of all, is that you as a boxer learn that the other person in the ring also has achieved a tremendous goal, for he has mastered the same difficult tasks you have. Maybe you are a bit better or perhaps he has perfected his skills more. It makes no difference. Both of you have achieved enough strength, savvy, and skill to box with each other.

Out of such knowledge comes deep respect for the other fellow. Have you ever watched on TV or in person an amateur boxing match—possibly one between teams from different countries—and seen the boxers embrace after it is over? That is not just for show. Boxing builds brotherhood.

The ring is a very good place to get to know others. Boxing can bring boys from very different backgrounds together. Whether they are rich or poor, whatever their race, if they are from city, country, or suburb, it makes no difference in the ring. There you stand on your own merits, and that is how you are judged, by yourself as well as others.

Equipment and Rules

Just as boxing has changed since the days of bare-fisted brawls, the equipment used in the sport has evolved. The bare-knuckle fighters of old battled in uniforms resembling tights and, of course, without gloves. The boxer of today wears shorts, often brightly colored, over an athletic supporter and protective cup, although you need only the supporter until you actually begin boxing with someone else, and you can practice in gym shorts and a T-shirt. Professional boxers, and amateurs who can afford them, wear boxing shoes of light leather, shin-high to prevent the ankle from twisting. Many amateur boxers, however, use tennis shoes, which are perfect for the exercises and drills in this book.

The most obvious piece of equipment, certainly, is the boxing glove. The boxing glove is made of leather on the outside and lined with cloth within. A layer of padding lies between the outer and inner surfaces. Padding is usually made from the hair of an animal such as a goat or horse, or foam rubber or a similar man-made material. Gloves are classified in terms of weight—the total of padding and the other materials of which they are made. The weight of gloves can vary according to the rules governing a boxing match. Major amateur boxing in this country usually uses ten-ounce gloves.

The type of boxing gloves you will need for the purposes of this book are called training gloves. They are much more heavily padded than gloves for matches. The padding reduces the impact of blows. Training gloves can weigh twelve, fourteen, or sixteen ounces.

Always try to use gloves of good quality. Inexpensive gloves often wear out quickly. They become tattered and frayed, making it possible for bits of worn leather to detach and enter another boxer's eye. Better quality gloves can be expensive, up to thirty or forty dollars a pair. So if you own a good pair take care of them. Keep them supple and clean with a leather soap. Store them hung up by the laces. Don't let them lie on the floor or any other place where they could become gritty.

Boxers do not simply put their bare hands into the gloves. The hand is wrapped with cloth. Wrappings for a match are of gauze, for practice of heavier cloth. The purpose of the wrapping is to prevent injury to the hand.

The hand wrappings you will need to practice the techniques in this book can be bought or ordered through most large sporting goods stores for a few dollars. They are of white

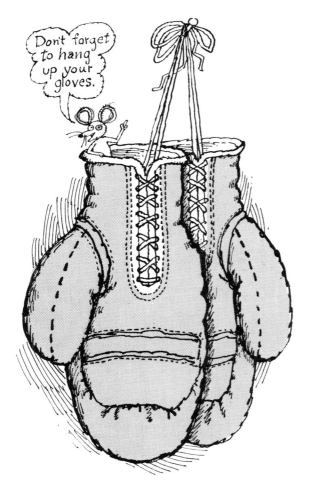

cloth, two inches wide, and about eight feet long. At one end of a wrapping is a loop, at the other a pair of ties. The loop goes around your thumb, while the ties are fastened together to secure the wrapping.

Details on how to wrap your hand—a most important measure—are shown in the drawings. Learn to wrap your hands properly before putting on the gloves. The wrappings should feel snug but not too tight. You do not want to cut off blood circulation to your hand. If you feel "pins and needles" in your hand after wrapping it, take the wrapping off and put it back on more loosely.

Boxers wear rubber mouthpieces to protect their teeth and lips. Boxing mouthpieces usually cover only the upper teeth. Those often provided to football players cover both the upper and lower. While you will not actually be landing punches as far as this book is concerned, when you practice with your partner you should wear a mouthpiece in case a blow strikes by accident. Besides, if you plan on going further in boxing, you will need to get used to the feel of the mouthpiece while you are in the ring. Before using a mouthpiece rinse it in hot water and then oral antiseptic.

After your hands are wrapped, put on the

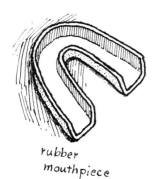

rubber
mouthpiece

34

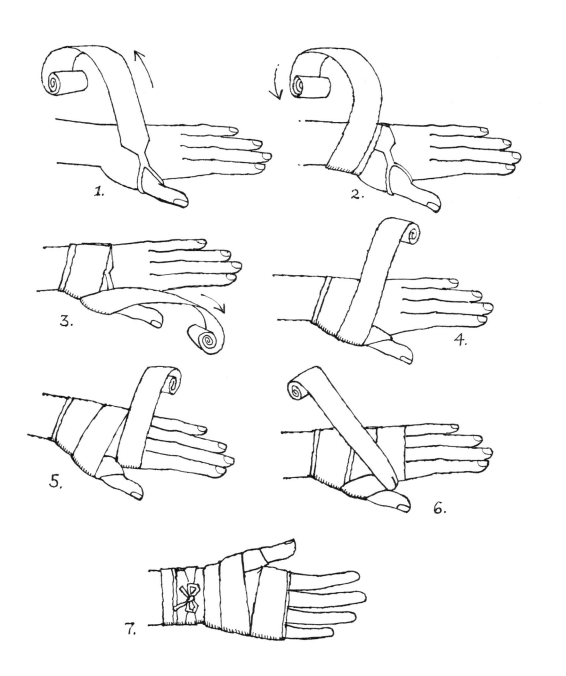

1.

2.

3.

4.

5.

6.

7.

gloves. Make sure your hands are inserted as deeply as possible into the gloves. Lace them firmly but not too tightly. Have your partner wrap the ends of the laces around your wrist and tie them on the back of the wrist so they will not come loose and get into someone's eye. You may want to keep the laces securely wrapped by covering their ends with a strip of adhesive tape.

If you go on to box in a club, you will find that during practice rounds boxers usually wear headgear. The training headgear is padded around the front, sides, and rear of the head, over the eyes, ears, and sides of the jaw. It takes the shock of blows and protects against cuts.

RULES

Early in your career as an amateur boxer, you will have to learn the rules of the sport. They differ slightly among various boxing organizations and tournaments, but for the most part they are similar. You can best learn them by studying the rulebooks provided by boxing groups, which your coach should have. Ask him questions when you have them, which for sure you will. If some of the rules sound very technical, don't worry. If he is a good coach, he will be able to explain them clearly.

Just for your information, however, here are some basic guidelines to amateur boxing rules. The most important rules cover fouls, which are not just unfair moves, but dangerous ones. Especially bad fouls are hitting behind the neck or below the waist, striking someone who is down, butting with your head, and using your knee to strike. You are not allowed to hit with a forearm or elbow or to punch an

Some very <u>foul</u> boxing behavior

opponent while pulling him toward you.

Boxers are matched according to weight. There are many weight classes in amateur boxing, to give a large number of boxers a chance. The classes differ slightly from one tournament to the next. As a guide, however, here are weight classes that have been used by the AAU. The weights given are the maximum for each class.

LIGHT FLYWEIGHT—106 POUNDS

FLYWEIGHT—112 POUNDS

BANTAMWEIGHT—119 POUNDS

FEATHERWEIGHT—125 POUNDS

LIGHTWEIGHT—132 POUNDS

LIGHT WELTERWEIGHT—139 POUNDS

WELTERWEIGHT—147 POUNDS

LIGHT MIDDLEWEIGHT—156 POUNDS

MIDDLEWEIGHT—165 POUNDS

LIGHT HEAVYWEIGHT—178 POUNDS

HEAVYWEIGHT—MORE THAN 178 POUNDS

To box in a given weight class, you must be of no more than the maximum poundage allowed for it and more than the maximum for the class below. The classes given above are for boxers sixteen years of age and over. There are different classes for younger boys, starting below 100 pounds.

SCORING

Boxing matches are supervised by the third man in the ring, the referee. He can stop a match if he thinks one of the boxers stands a chance of being hurt. He also enforces the rules—watching for fouls, for instance.

Scoring is by rounds. Based on the scoring rules that have been used in AAU bouts, the winner of a round gets twenty points. The loser can receive any amount less than that. Even if a boxer is doing very poorly, he usually never receives less than fifteen or sixteen points for a round he manages to finish.

Amateur bouts usually have three rounds. In most tournaments, rounds are two minutes each, although there are exceptions. Major championships and contests on an international level have three-minute rounds. In Junior Olympics, boxers ten and eleven years of age go for one-minute rounds, while those of twelve and thirteen years box for rounds of a minute and a half each.

The beginning and end of a round is signalled by the sound of a bell or gong, although sometimes a buzzer or whistle is used. The first time you enter the ring for an organized match and hear the bell clang for the opening round, it may seem like the loudest sound you ever have heard. Welcome it, because the bell is opening up a new experience that you will remember for the rest of your life. From then on, you can call yourself a boxer.

First Get in Shape

It is a bad idea to play or practice any sport before your body is in shape for it—that is, prepared with strong, flexible muscles and plenty of endurance so you do not get out of breath. This is especially true of a contact sport like boxing. If you are not in shape, you are much more likely to get hurt. Trying to box without preparing your body is like taking a difficult test in school without studying first.

Boxing takes lots of stamina. A boxer's legs and endurance, or wind, should be as good as those of an experienced runner. He must be able to absorb blows like a football player. He must be as quick as a wrestler. His arms must be strong like those of a gymnast.

The way to build up your body for boxing is through exercise and, of course, good health habits, including the right amount of sleep and a proper diet. The program of exercises that follow will help you to get in shape. Even if you decide not to continue boxing, you may want to keep up the exercises so your body stays strong.

You should plan to do the series of daily exercises for at least a week before you begin to work on stance and footwork and punches. Your stomach should not be full of food or drink, even water. Exercising on a full stomach may make you sick. Early morning is a good time to exercise. Another is late in the afternoon, before supper. Whenever you exercise, however, do so at least an hour after a big meal.

When choosing a place to exercise, pick a

room that does not have furniture that will get in your way. Wear loose clothing, such as a sweat shirt, or T-shirt, and shorts. Wear sneakers, or exercise in your stocking feet.

Start slowly, especially if exercises such as these are new to you. If you get tired, rest for a moment. Above all, stop if you begin to feel weak and do not start again until your strength returns. You should build your muscles gradually. You can strain a muscle if you try to make it do too much at first. Keep in mind that it is better to do an exercise fewer times but carefully than many times sloppily.

EXERCISES

Loosening Up   Start your daily program with loosening-up exercises. These should precede any other exercises or boxing practices. If you don't, your muscles may cramp. Try this loosening-up exercise first: Stand in place. Your back should be straight but not stiff, your feet slightly apart, your arms at your sides. Relax. With your arms straight but relaxed—don't lock your elbows—shake your hands and wrists. Continue for thirty seconds, rest a moment, then repeat.

Rest a few more seconds. Now start to loosen up your shoulders. First revolve your arms at your sides in large circles. Don't stiffen your arms. Always move them in a relaxed fashion. Keep up the revolutions for a minute. Rest for a moment. Now extend your arms in front of your body and move your hands in small circles, again for a minute. Remember to rest if you are tired. Walk about a bit if you feel like it.

The next exercise will loosen up your neck muscles. Place your hands on your hips. Roll your head toward your right shoulder, but do not stop at that point. Keep your head moving in a circle. Your eyes will look at the floor, then over your right shoulder, and finally at the ceiling, until your head reaches the position from which it started. Do this exercise ten times. Rest a few seconds. Then do it ten more times, rolling your head toward your left shoulder.

You can loosen up your torso with a similar exercise, except this time you bend at the waist and move your whole upper body in a circle. Really stretch. It's good for you. Do this exercise ten times.

Jumping Jacks Now you have finished loosening up. It is time to begin building up your body with other exercises. Stand in a loose position of "attention." Raise up on your toes and jump, spreading your feet apart while swinging your arms overhead. Your palms should touch at the same time as you land—always on your toes—on the floor. Now jump back to the position from which you started. Try to do twenty-five of these movements, about one per second. If you cannot, work up to that number. This exercise, the jumping jack, strengthens the legs and improves the coordination of the feet.

Punching Exercise Stand in a crouch. With your hands in fists, move your arms in a punching motion, working them as hard as you can. Keep it up for ten seconds. Rest ten seconds. Do it again. Practice until you can do this exercise ten times. The punching exercise strengthens your arms and chest and increases your endurance.

Chest Pull Stand with your feet slightly spread, your arms at your sides, and your hands in fists. Extend your arms in front of you. Pull backward with both arms as hard as you can. Repeat the exercise ten times. If

you do this exercise right, you should feel a slight tug in your shoulders. The chest pull loosens and strengthens your arms and shoulders.

Neck Bridge Lie on your back with your hands folded together on your chest, your knees up, and your feet planted firmly on the floor close to your body. Using your head and feet, arch your body off the floor. Return to your original position and rest ten seconds. Repeat the exercise, working up to a maximum of ten. The strong neck muscles which this exercise builds are better able to absorb the shock of blows to the head.

Leg Lifts   Lie on the floor with your legs out-
stretched and your arms at your sides. Keeping your knees straight, raise your legs six
inches off the floor. Hold them in that position
for ten seconds. Lower your legs and rest for
ten seconds. This is a difficult exercise, but
an important one—it builds up your stomach
and leg muscles. It may take you a while before you are strong enough to do it ten times.

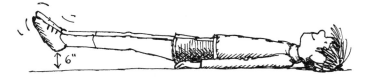

Sit-Ups   Lie on the floor with your legs out-
stretched and your hands behind your head
or against the back of your neck. Can you sit
up without moving your feet or legs? If not,
you need this exercise, another builder of
stomach muscles. Do it ten times.

Push-Ups Lie on your stomach. Place your palms on the floor, one hand under each shoulder. With your body straight as a board, raise yourself to arm's length. Your weight should rest on your hands and toes. Then lower yourself back toward the floor, but don't quite touch it. Starting with as many push-ups as you can do without straining, work toward ten, more if you can. Do the push-ups as fast as possible. They build punching power.

Running for the Ring   Running is the single best exercise for boxers. Boxers call running exercise "roadwork." This does not mean you really have to run on roads, although many boxers do. A running track or a path through a park are best. Hard pavements can cause unnecessary muscle pains.

If you do your roadwork regularly you won't run out of breath easily in the ring. Nor will your legs weaken. Roadwork, moreover, helps tone up your whole body, as jogging does. Except that roadwork is not the same as jogging. A jogger covers a long distance at the same speed, usually at a slow pace. Roadwork means running as fast as you can for a time, then slowing down for a while before picking up the pace again. Running this way prepares the body for bursts of activity in the ring.

Unless you are used to running, try only a little roadwork in the beginning. Run with all your might for thirty seconds. Then walk quickly for a minute. Count the minutes off in your head if you do not have a friend with a watch or clock to time you. How do you feel after the first two minutes? If you're not winded, try the series again. Remember, however, do not start roadwork until you have done your loosening-up exercises.

Experienced boxers run miles daily. If you can build up to a quarter-hour of roadwork a day, it will be enough for the level of boxing in this book. Alternate running hard for two minutes with a minute of trotting. After you have developed your wind, you may want to run at a quick pace for the last five minutes.

Boxers do roadwork rain or shine, in cold or warm weather. If the weather is unpleasant, dress warmly and wear a cap to keep your head dry. Wear a sweatshirt over an undershirt in cool weather, and a jacket over both when it is really cold. Make sure you have gloves on your hands and a knitted cap on your head in freezing temperatures.

You do not need fancy running shoes for roadwork. If you have them, fine, but tennis

shoes—"sneakers"—are good enough. The shoes should be securely laced, but not so tight that they hurt.

After you can do your roadwork without becoming exhausted, you may want to give it a different twist. You can use it to strengthen your arms as well as your legs. Carry weights in your hand when you run. I know one young boxer who used to run holding a full soup can in each fist.

Skipping Rope Skipping rope is a tried-and-true boxing exercise. It builds up your legs and wind. Do it for about five minutes a day.

The rope should be long enough so that you can stand on it with both feet and hold the ends at your waist. The technique for skipping is to step over the rope one foot at a time, on your toes, as fast as you can. If you never have done it before, you will have to practice slowly at first. When you are proficient, you even can try tricks, like skipping with the rope crossed in front of you.

AFTER YOU ARE IN SHAPE

Once you are in shape, you do not have to do all the exercises described above every day. You might exercise for five minutes or so before you begin your punching drills. Remember, however, to always to do the loosening-up exercises before anything else. If you can run daily, it will be very good for you. But three or four times a week are enough.

Stance and Footwork

While the fist strikes a punch and the arm delivers it, most of the force should come from your body. A blow with just the power of the arm behind it is very weak compared to one backed by the body. This is why two of the most important things in boxing are stance and footwork—knowing how to position your body and how to move it around the ring, from one place to another. The secret of punching powerfully and accurately lies in stance and footwork.

THE STANCE

Over the years, boxers have developed a basic stance from which the arms, legs, eyes, head, shoulders, and all other parts of the body important to boxing work together, smoothly and in balance.

It may take you a little time to learn it, but once you do, taking the proper stance becomes automatic. Experienced boxers often create their own individual versions of the basic stance. Most good fighters, however, never add their own touches until they have truly mastered the fundamental position.

As mentioned earlier, the modern boxing stance is a variation of the stance of the fencer, or swordsman. Again, the difference is that the swordsman held his weapon in his right hand, in front of him, whereas modern boxers keep the right hand back over the right foot, with the left hand "leading" in front. (The descriptions given here are for right-handers.

Left-handed readers will keep the left hand over the left foot, with the right hand leading.) The reason is that for most boxers the right hand delivers the most powerful punch. To get the body fully behind the right, the fist should be carried back and launched from there.

Positioning Your Feet and Trunk The basic stance depends first and foremost on the position of your feet and trunk. Stand straight, with your arms at your sides and your feet parallel and slightly apart. With your left foot take one step forward. Move it only the distance you normally take for a step. As you step, shift your weight to your left foot. If you do it properly, your right knee will bend slightly and your heel will rise slightly from the floor.

Next turn your left foot so the toe points a quarter turn to the right. Turning at the waist—with your arms still loosely hanging at

your sides—shift your body so your left shoulder is in line with your left heel. Do not move
your head, but keep looking straight in front

of you. In other words, the left side of your body forms a straight line, from shoulder to heel. Keep your body loose, remember, with your left knee relaxed but not bent. If you feel uncomfortable—if you are slightly off balance—experiment by moving your right foot a few inches to the right, but *not* back.

If you are in the correct position, your feet should be directly under your body. Your trunk should be straight, not bent at the waist, and the back of your head should be in line with your right side. In this stance you have control over your body balance. That is the key to boxing. Controlled balance lets you put weight behind punches and lets you move away from your opponent's blows smoothly and quickly.

With the help of a friend, you can test to see if you have the right balance in your stance. Assume the position described so far, making sure your right heel is slightly up from the floor. Have your friend outstretch his hand

and give you a push on your left shoulder or chest—it should be a sharp push, but not a huge shove. If you are positioned right, the push will not dislodge your feet. Your weight will go back on your right heel, preserving your balance.

Positioning Your Arms Once you have learned how to position your feet and trunk, it is time to put the arms in place. With your left arm at your side and your hand loosely clenched, raise the forearm until your fist is level with your left shoulder.

In boxing there is only one way to make a fist. Close the fingers into the palm, folding the thumb across the other four fingers. The first joint of the thumb should rest over the first knuckle of the index and third fingers. You should clench the fist firmly, but there is no need to squeeze hard. You will only tire your hand. Making a fist any other way leads to trouble. If you fold your thumb inside your

fingers you risk breaking it when you strike the target. Always keep your arm, wrist, and fist in a straight line. If you turn your wrists, holding the fist at an angle to your arm, you could break wrist bones.

Hold your forearm so that the folded thumb faces right, the knuckles are straight up, and the elbow is pointed toward the floor. Then move your left fist out away from the shoulder about ten inches. The upper part of your left arm should be near your body, but not held tightly against it.

Next, position your right arm. Moving the forearm, bring the right hand to shoulder level. Keep the elbow close to the ribs. Leave your hand partly open and turn the palm so it faces slightly outward. To make sure your right hand is held at the proper height, try this. Slide it nine or ten inches left. Does it touch your body just to right of the left shoulder? If so, move it back to its original place. That is where you should hold it.

How to Hold Your Head　All that remains for you to know about the basic stance is how to hold your head. Without leaning forward, drop your chin so it touches your body near the left collarbone. Does your neck feel strained or otherwise uncomfortable? If so, then you are bending your head farther than you need to. You should feel relaxed and loose. Your head should be tilted forward just enough so the top of it and your forehead are facing in the direction where an opponent would stand. This way, the only target for the opponent is the hard part of your head. He has to work to get a glove into your face.

A boxer who sticks to the basic stance exposes very little of his body to an opponent. The ribs lie behind the elbows and the "V" formed by each arm. The arms, if relaxed, can move to cover any part of the trunk. Held high, the hands are ready to ward off blows to the head. The entire body, moreover, offers only its side to the opponent, like the edge of a knife. If, on the other hand, the boxer were squared off against his opponent, face-to-face, the full front of his body would be an easy target.

When you finally box from the basic stance, here is something important to remember: never bend from the waist to reach an opponent shorter than you. Once you bend the top half of your body forward, you lose your height advantage and come in range of punches that otherwise would not reach you.

FOOTWORK

Before you learn how to punch, you need to have your footwork down pat—that is, you should be able to move your feet to position the body to its best advantage—and to do it in a flash. The better your footwork, the less chance that you will be caught out of position to either attack or escape an opponent.

A boxer with good footwork owns the ring.

A boxer with good footwork owns the ring. He travels quickly and smoothly around it. He can glide from one part to another, as he wishes. He is at home in any part of the territory within the ropes and is able to move out of danger or away from attack at anytime.

He can move all around an opponent, striking where least expected. Even if the other man is stronger, and hits harder, the fighter with the best footwork often has a great edge.

Footwork does not have to be fancy. You do not have to be in constant motion. All you have to do is move your feet well enough so that your body is properly set and you are the one in command of the ring, keeping yourself in the best part of it for whatever you want to do. If, for example, two steps will cut off an opponent who is trying to escape from a corner, that is all you need. You definitely do not need a spectacular shuffle, or showy dancing. Muhammad Ali popularized the lightning razzle-dazzle of his feet that became known as the "Ali Shuffle." But you can be sure that long before Ali tried his shuffle, he perfected his standard footwork. Some young boxers who try fancy footwork—or for that matter showy moves of any kind—never learn the basics. It keeps them from reaching their full potential.

In the long run, the feet are as important to a boxer as the hands that strike the blows. Hands and feet must move together, as different parts of the same machine. The movement of one part must be coordinated with the other. You need to move fast when necessary, yet you also need to have your feet set at all times, never out of balance and always ready to change position.

The Advance The first kind of footwork to learn is how to advance. By the way, it is easier to practice footwork on a smooth surface. A wood floor, for instance, is better than a thick rug. If you can, use such a floor.

Take your stance. Remember, stay loose. Your knees should be relaxed but not deeply bent. With the "knife edge" of your body, face the spot where your opponent would be. Make sure your left foot is flat on the floor, your right heel raised slightly. Now slide your left foot forward about half its length. Don't worry about speed now. Try for form. Follow up by bringing your right foot forward a couple of inches. You should end up in exactly the position from which you started. Except for the raised right heel, at no time during the move should your feet have broken contact with the floor.

As you advanced, you essentially kept your basic stance and, by maintaining foot contact with the floor, your balance. Your body was in position at all times.

Try this move again, this time a bit more quickly. Take it one move at a time. After you have brought up your right foot, stop to check if you have kept your basic stance. Continue to practice the move until it feels comfortable. Make sure you stop to check your stance each time you complete one move.

Once your body feels at ease with a single advance move, advance with three or four before stopping. Is your body's "knife edge" forward? If not, you are in a position that

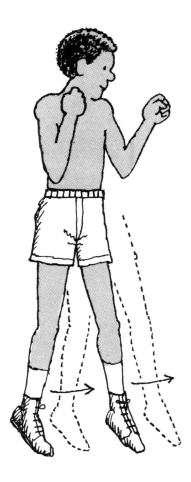

would make you a tempting target. In a boxing match, you probably would run into some punches.

Don't worry if you have to spend a lot of time to get the moves down pat. In fact, before building up speed, wait until your body has picked up a rhythm that you can feel as you advance. Once you have the "feel" of the move, quickness comes naturally. Practice until you can move with ease from one end of the room to the other.

The Retreat It is no shame for a boxer to retreat, either to back off from too many punches or to draw in—or "sucker"—an opponent into advancing too quickly, leaving him open to blows. Retreating can be a form of attack as well as an escape.

The move used to retreat is the opposite of the one you learned for advancing. From your basic stance, move your right foot backward a few inches. Is your toe on the floor

72

and your heel raised? Unless they are, you will be off balance. Next, bring your left foot back so you are in your original position again. That is all there is to it. Except now you should repeat the move until you can do it automatically.

Advance and Retreat   Starting again in the basic stance, put together your moves for advancing and retreating. At first, advance once, then retreat once. Again, when you have developed a rhythm with both these moves, increase and vary the number of moves forward and backward.

Circling   Now that you have learned to advance and retreat in a straight line, remember this: It is all right to move this way when you are first learning, but a smart boxer seldom travels in a straight line for more than a few steps, especially when retreating. Imagine that you are boxing an opponent and are retreating in a straight line all across the ring. Your opponent merely has to follow you closely enough to keep within punching distance. In actual boxing, unless you really have your opponent on the run and want to stay on him, circling is better than straight movement.

Suppose you want to circle to the right about an opponent. You have a choice of two methods. The one I like best begins when you move your right foot, heel up, in a sweeping step that travels in front of and around your opponent—almost a quarter turn. Then you bring up your left foot into the starting position. You will find, when you begin boxing, that this move will bring you to your opponent's side. His hands will still be aimed straight ahead, away from you. Both of yours will be in range of him. Circling to the right keeps you away from your opponent's right hand, usually his power punch.

Here is the other way to circle right. Start

Circling to the right with the right foot

from your regular stance. Step across your body with your left foot, then as quickly as you can bring your right foot behind it until you end up in the basic stance once more. Go through the same movement again, but remember, take it slowly at first.

Decide on the method of circling right that feels most comfortable, and learn that one first. Then practice the other way, for you never know when you might want to use it while boxing. Practice slowly until you can circle smoothly, then increase your speed a little at a time. Keep practicing until you can circle easily and rapidly, as naturally as if you were going for a walk. Then learn to circle left.

Before trying to circle left, think of your left foot as the point of a compass—the kind you use for drawing circles, not the kind for finding directions. Starting from your stance, slide your left foot, or "compass point," six inches to the left. Stop. Now, with your left

Circling to the right with the left foot

quick two-step to the left

1.
2.

foot in place, swing your body around until you are in the basic stance again. If you do it correctly, you will sweep past and to the side of your opponent's right.

You can also move left with a quick two-step, although it takes you more sideways than in a circle. From your stance, slide your left foot about six inches farther left, moving your right foot back into place behind it. As the right foot moves, keep your heel up and your toe touching the floor. When moving in any direction, for that matter, try not to be caught with either foot off the floor. This unbalances you, leaving you in a bad position to either throw or escape a punch.

Putting It All Together   Once you can do each of the movements more easily than you ever thought possible, put them together. Try advancing, circling left, retreating, stepping to the left, circling right. Mix the moves in as many different combinations as you like.

At all times be sure to hold your hands in the basic position—relaxed but ready.

The proper stance and footwork enable you to be the master of the ring—to move in for the attack, to escape your opponent if need be, and in general to keep a step ahead of him, so he will have to react to you. A boxer goes a long way toward winning if he can follow the rule, "Be first."

Once you are able to assume your stance and move your feet without having to really think about every action, you are ready to learn to use your hands. And, as with footwork, learning to punch starts with slow, careful repetitions that will develop into automatic actions.

Start Punching the Right Way

Maybe you have seen two people get angry at each other and start a fist fight. Chances are that most of their punches relied on arm power alone and were swung in wide arcs. Few brawlers really know how to punch. It's a good thing, too, because poorly thrown punches do not do the damage of those thrown properly. A punch gets power, as we have said, from the body—and also when it travels in a straight line. The shorter the distance the punch travels, moreover, the better. Not only does the punch arrive quickly, but

some of the hardest punches in boxing, or karate, for that matter, travel only a few inches
before landing.

There are many different blows in boxing.
Each one has a purpose. Each is done in a
particular way. It takes time to learn the right
way to carry out each type of punch. But the
right way is by far the best.

USING THE BODY

Imagine, for a moment, the way a woodcutter chops down a tree. When he swings the
axe, his body is balanced on his feet and he
twists at the waist. The weight of his body
backs up the downswing.

Suppose he swings the axe with only his
arms. His swing might not even have enough
force to make the axehead bite into the bark.
It is much the same with punches that don't
have the weight of the body behind them.

This does not mean you should heave your whole body into every punch. You can call on your body's force by just twisting your waist, shifting a shoulder, or sliding your feet a few inches.

When a woodcutter chops, he does not aim only at the bark on the outside of the tree. He drives his axe forcefully, trying to sink it deeply into the wood. In the same way, you should drive your punch through its target, not just try to hit it. Would you try to swat a baseball and not follow through with your swing? Not if you knew what you were doing. Well, following through is just as important for good punching.

Another thing to remember is that a punch is very different from a push. A well-thrown punch means business. It explodes with force. Snap it forward with a burst of power—as much as you can pack into a split second. In other words, a punch should really be "power packed," in every sense of the word. It is true

82

that some kinds of punches have more force than others. Each blow you land should have as much power as you can give it—but throw it quickly.

How quickly? You may be surprised. A trained boxer, with fast hands, can land a punch faster than a rattlesnake can strike— not just a little but many times faster. And that is not all. There is a good chance that after just a little practice, you will be able to strike a blow faster than a rattlesnake darts at its victim.

Maybe you still do not really believe it. Then you might be interested to learn what happened several years ago at the Denver Museum of Natural History in Colorado. A scientist there measured the speed of a striking rattler and found that the head of the snake travels at about eight feet per second. That is fast, to be sure, but when the scientist timed how quickly he could throw a punch called the left jab, he discovered he

was faster. His fist moved at 18.1 feet per second. The scientist did not know how to box, so you can just imagine the speed of a good boxer's jab. It makes a rattlesnake look slow.

Maybe there is no need to warn you, but just in case you happen to meet a rattlesnake someday, keep in mind that a jab may be quicker, but rattlers are still pretty tough characters. I have been a zoo curator as well as a boxer, and I can tell you that it is a lot less risky to box for fun than it is to play around with rattlesnakes.

You even can learn something about boxing

from a rattlesnake. When the snake strikes, it shoots straight at its target. Remember, a straight line is the shortest distance between two points. The best punches in boxing take advantage of this fact, whether they come at the target from the front, side, or below.

Imagine that you and your opponent both start a punch at the same time. He swings one wide. You throw one straight. His will still be whistling through the air when yours bops him on the nose. He may have quicker hands than you do, but if he swings wide and you move your fist straight ahead, you will land first. If you happen to be near a boxer's corner during a regular bout, in fact, you may hear his coach or trainer urging him to "be first, be first!"

A wide swing has another disadvantage. It is easy for an opponent to escape a blow thrown that way. You will learn about the various defenses against punches later. For now, however, remember that no punch is easier to block or evade than one coming at you wide.

1.

2.

The WIDE SWINGER gets it on the Nose

3.

THE LEFT JAB

The left jab is not the hardest punch in boxing—far from it—but it is the most important.
Boxers have won many matches by relying
almost entirely on the left jab.

The left jab has several purposes. It can be
your best defense, for if you use it correctly,
your opponent will be continually off balance.
It is a key part of offense. Although the jab
is for most boxers a light punch, it can sting
and back up an opponent, it can set up other
types of punches, and it can score points when
it lands.

A bit later on, you will learn that in boxing,
punches are thrown in series, called "combinations." Each time you complete a punch,
you should be set to throw another, either
with the other or the same hand, if you have
the chance.

For now, however, you should work at
learning a single left jab, or "jab," as it is com-

monly called. Get into your stance, relax, but be ready. In the beginning, the moves you make should be very slow and a bit exaggerated, to give you the feel, or rhythm of things. Once you get it, then you can sharpen your style, punching faster and with less movement.

If you have taken your stance properly, your left fist will be about shoulder height, with the knuckles facing left. (Remember, if you are a left-hander, do everything with the hand opposite from the one mentioned in the text.) Extend your arm to its fullest. As your arm moves outward, turn your wrist so the knuckles and back of your hand face upward by the time your arm is straight. This is how your arm and fist should be positioned when the jab strikes its target, the head of your opponent. There is, however, more to the jab than that.

Starting from the basic stance, use what you learned about footwork to advance. As your left foot moves forward, you shove off on your right foot and extend your arm in the jab. The jab should be all the way out at about the time your left foot stops and your right foot—toe touching the floor—comes up into place again. The punch travels straight, at about shoulder height or just a little higher. As soon as the jab has struck—in this case an imaginary target—bring your fist back to its starting position. Don't yank it back. Just let it come back naturally toward the shoulder. Whatever you do, make sure that as you bring it back, your fist stays at shoulder height. If you get in the habit of bringing your fist back low, when you actually begin boxing you will have given your opponent an opening to hit you.

Try advancing and jabbing three or four times. Then stop. This time, jab and advance once. As you return your fist, retreat one step. Now try this: Jab and advance. Jab and retreat. Jab and advance. Jab and retreat. Go slowly,

1.

2.

3.

The
Left Jab

and work on rhythm. Next try moving ahead a few times, then retreating, or going forward and backward as you like.

No drill in boxing is more important than learning the jab. Practice it as often as you can. Keep snapping the jab out there.

You may notice that when you advance a step and jab, your left shoulder turns slightly to the right. This is where the weight of the body comes from. Eventually, you will be able to put weight into the jab without advancing at all. You will be able to do it simply by twisting your upper body so your shoulder moves right as your arm extends.

Actually, experienced boxers often start the jab and other blows by moving their hips and shoulders a fraction of a second before the arm. This gets even more power behind the punch. It requires lots of coordination, however, so is one of the tricks you can learn later, if you decide to get involved with organized boxing.

You may be coordinated enough to fall into the rhythm of twisting your body and jabbing right from the start. If not, no matter. You can learn by jabbing and advancing, each time shortening the forward step. Finally, when you are moving forward only a fraction of an inch, you will find that you are practically jabbing in place, while still keeping the rhythm and power behind the punch.

For a moment, go back to jabbing slowly. Extend your arm, but don't bring it back. Keep your fist out there. Where is your chin in relation to the shoulder? If your chin is above your shoulder, out in the open, you are jabbing too low. When you jab properly, the shoulder ends up covering the chin. This is not because you have dropped your chin— never do that. It is because the shoulder has moved up in front of the chin. A jab also can be thrown while you are retreating, although to do it right and at the same time maintain your balance is difficult. The arm moves outward at the same time as the left foot slides backward. Jabbing this way helps keep an opponent who is going after you from landing serious punches—if you keep the jab in his face. But this is difficult and really something that you may not learn to do well unless you join an organized boxing program.

Jabs can also be thrown while you are circling, especially while circling to the left. It is a matter of throwing the jab while the left foot moves sideward, instead of forward.

DRILLING WITH A PARTNER

Once you are comfortable throwing the jab alone, you are ready for a jabbing drill with a partner. The drill will give you practice in aiming your punches at a target—in this instance an open glove—and will help you to learn timing. Each of you should wear a rubber mouthpiece, in case one of you misses the target and accidentally hits the other in the face. The mouthpiece will protect the teeth.

Take the drills seriously. Don't get silly and fool around, and never *try* to land a punch to your partner's head or body.

You and your partner should face each other in the basic stance. Position yourself with your left foot just inside his, so your left hand is between both of his. Your partner should stand facing you and in the same position as you. If you can keep this position while boxing, your left hand will always be between his power hand, the right, and your chin.

To begin the jabbing drill, your partner should hold up his right glove, open and near his face—not too close, though, or he might be hit. You jab at the glove, moving in whatever way you wish, while your partner stands in place. Are you following through with the jab? If so, your partner's gloved hand should be jarred backward. In fact, his hand should

94

sting if your jab is as snappy as it should be.

As you improve, your partner should move his glove, from side to side and up and down. Take turns with your partner, letting him jab at your glove.

LEAD WITH A LEFT

The left jab is the first type of punch most boxers learn, and the one they use most in the ring. There is a reason for this: the jab is a blow that often leads to others, which are more powerful than it is.

The moment you land a jab and pull it back, your weight shifts from the left to the right side of your body. This means that your weight is ready to be launched behind the right. So the jab naturally can lead into a blow with the right hand—the straight right.

The next chapter tells how to use the straight right after the left, as well as the way to deliver other types of blows, alone and in combinations.

More
Punches and Combinations

In actual bouts, punches are seldom thrown by themselves. Good boxers know how to use several different punches, one after another, in various combinations. A left jab followed by a straight right is a combination, although a very simple one. As with the individual punches in a series, one set of combinations builds upon another, the aim being to put your opponent at a disadvantage and to score points.

In this chapter you can begin by learning the straight right that will follow the left lead.

Then you will move on to some other, slightly more complicated blows. Finally, you will read how to put all of them together.

THE STRAIGHT RIGHT

As a rule, the straight right is the hardest punch a right-hander delivers. It can be used to the head or body. Some people think that a straight right starts way back, and gathers force as the arm moves from a bent to an extended position. Actually, a straight right can travel just a few inches and land with terrific force. I have seen boxers knocked out cold by a right hand that moved only four or five inches.

Start by throwing a left jab and holding the arm extended. Twist your body to the right as before, only this time drive your right fist forward at the same time as you turn your body. The knuckles and back of your right

Left jab to straight right
combination

hand will turn so that when you arm is extended, they face the ceiling.

Try the combination slowly several times.
Make sure that as you turn you can feel your
balance shift and the force of your body
moving through your right shoulder down
your arm. Notice that as you punch with your

right, your left hand comes back. Don't forget that left. Keep the elbow close to the body and the fist high. It is your defense against a counterpunch by an opponent.

Now speed up your right a little. When you punch, strike with all you are worth. A right hand thrown properly is fierce, jolting. Hurl it forward. Put as much into it as you would when making a game-saving tackle in football. If there is a time in boxing to let loose, it is when you unleash your right. Never, however, lose your cool.

LEFT-RIGHT DRILLS

The position of your partner's glove in a left-right drill is the same as for the left jab. First practice the one-two combination—that is what it is—against his open right glove. It will take you several days to build your coordination to the point where you can perform the combination smoothly.

Almost as if you were in slow motion, throw the jab, then twisting at the hips, follow up with the right. You may find at first that you are concentrating so much on the left that it zings in, but the right follows so weakly it seems hardly able to dent a powder puff. This often happens to beginners. Or else they may think so much about getting power into the right they may hardly peck with the left. Sometimes it can take several days to break this bad habit, which even may return from time to time. But by keeping a clear head, and not worrying too much, you can beat it.

Here's how. As you jab, forcefully, but for now slowly, count off to yourself, "one." Keep the jab out there, touching the open glove, and continue the count with, "and." Return the left hand, throwing the right, to the count of, "two."

Each beat—including the "and"—should have equal time. Keep counting as you slowly punch, "One and two. One and two." If you concentrate on each count fully, you will de-

Left-Right Drill

velop what boxers call "timing." It is another key to knowing how to punch.

As you practice, speed up your count and your punching. Before too long, you will not need to count, because the right rhythm will have become automatic.

By now, you probably are beginning to feel a bit like a real boxer, and that, in fact, is what you are becoming. You also may be learning that moving around and punching for even a minute or so can be very good exercise. Boxing involves so much movement that you condition your body while you practice your skills. That's one of the things that makes boxing fun.

THE TWO-MINUTE ROUND

Do you think you could work in the ring for a full round, the two-minute kind used in many amateur bouts? Next time you drill, try to last two two-minute rounds, with a one-minute rest in between. Maybe you have another friend who can time you and your partner with a clock or watch. If not, you will have to keep an eye on the time yourself.

Build up the number of rounds until you can drill for at least three without a long rest—and by a long rest I mean five or ten minutes. From now on, it is a good idea to time all of your punching drills.

HOOKS AND UPPERCUTS

The left jab and the straight right are the most basic blows, but they are only two of the many different types of punches in the arsenal of an experienced boxer. Among the others are punches that are used when a boxer and his opponent are at close quarters. Because they are done with the elbow bent, they do not have the reach of blows thrown with the arm extended—but they are very forceful.

One is the hook, the other the uppercut.

Hooks and uppercuts are more difficult to throw than straight punches. Many boxers, even experienced ones, never really learn the fundamentals of the hook and the uppercut. They merely swing their arm instead of using their body to propel it, an easy mistake to make with bent-arm punches.

THE LEFT HOOK

A friend of mine who is one of those amateurs who became a successful professional boxer had been fighting an opponent for three rounds. He was beating his man, but the fight was close. My friend was both a skillful boxer and fierce puncher. I expected him to knock his opponent out, before long. The bell rang for the next round. The two fighters met near the middle of the ring. The first thing my friend did was to lower his left shoulder, suddenly, as if he was going to punch the opponent's body.

He was trying to fake his opponent, and the move worked. The opponent dropped his right hand to protect his body. That was when my friend sent a high left hook to the man's jaw and knocked him out.

It all happened in just a second or two, and it showed how effective a left hook can be when used by a very good fighter. The left hook works very well with fakes and combina-

tions, and it has power. If a fighter knows how to throw it well, the punch is as much a threat as a straight right. In fact, the left hook can be a more dangerous punch than the right. When I was boxing in my college days, I never developed the power I should have had in my right. But my left hook seemed to come more naturally. I scored better with it than the right. I mention this only so you will see the importance of the left hook, and not so you will neglect your right hand.

I always have found it easier by far to throw a left hook after another move—such as a punch, block, or fake. A good boxer, however, should be able to use a hook at any time, including as a lead.

The important thing to remember about the left hook is that the arm stays bent all the way through the punch, even after the fist connects. I like to forget that it is an arm, but instead think of it as a bent club, whipped around from my shoulder.

All the power in a left hook comes from a sudden shift of weight from the left leg to the right. I do not think there is any other blow that shows so obviously the importance of weight to punching power.

An easy way to see this yourself is to start the left hook from the position you would be at after throwing a straight right.

Begin by taking your basic stance. Now let your right hand fly, holding it out instead of bringing it back. You will see that once you have followed through with the right, your left side is cocked, ready to punch. The trick is to release the weight on the left behind the hook.

To see how this is done, hold the position you assume after throwing the right. Now snap your right shoulder back, turning at the hips. The move should start your left shoulder forward, following the right. Your weight will begin shifting to the right as well. Don't finish the move at this point. Go back to the basic stance.

1. basic stance

2. throwing a right

3. left hook

So, from your basic stance, start practicing a hook in this way. Keeping your left arm in its starting position, snap your right shoulder back and let the left shoulder follow, while pivoting on your left toe. If you wish, think of the left foot as the compass point again. A split second after the left shoulder begins its move, release your left arm, which will naturally follow the shoulder. Make sure to keep it securely in the bent position. At the same time, however, raise your elbow, so that your arm will end up parallel to the floor. Let the arm go, still bent, as though you were trying

Snap
right
shoulder
back.

Keep
left
arm
bent.

Pivot on
left foot.

basic stance   left hook

to touch your right shoulder. Continue to pivot on your left foot, and follow through. Now stop. Is your weight over your right leg? Is your left arm across your body, your right hand and arm in close? Is your left heel up and pivoted outward? If so, you have completed the hook.

Of all punches, the left hook is the most difficult to perform smoothly. You will have to practice it slowly, and for a long time. Some fighters also use a right hook. You do not need this blow now, but you may want to learn it later.

Hook Drills The procedure for open glove drills with the left hook is the same as for other punches, except that the position of the target is different. Your partner, who is the "target," holds the glove with the palm facing left. The glove is held high for practicing left hooks to the head.

You also can hook to the body. The target should be held at chest or waist level. When you hook to the body, use the same technique as to the head, except that you bend at the knees while hooking. Bending at the knees gets you low enough for such body punches. Don't lower your head when you bend your knees but keep your eyes looking ahead.

UPPERCUTS

Uppercuts are punches best used when you are boxing close to your opponent. They are especially effective to the body. Work on your right uppercut first, as it has more force than the left.

When you throw a right uppercut, the force of it starts deep down in your right leg and explodes like a rocket heading for the sky—straight up. The power behind the punch comes from lowering the right side of the body slightly, then straightening it and twisting left. To make it easier, start by practicing the uppercut after a left hook. The position in which you end up after the hook is just right to launch the uppercut.

From your basic stance, throw the left hook and leave it out there. Now drop your right shoulder a bit more, keeping your bent right arm so close to your body that your elbow touches it. Your fist should be turned palm toward the ceiling. Now, start twisting your body to the left. At the same time bring up your shoulder and snap your right arm up, aiming it at the spot your opponent's mid-section or jaw would be in in a real match. Put

right uppercut

all your power into straightening up, and
"dig" with your arm. When practicing, your
fist should end up almost level with your eyes,
palm facing you. The follow-through is very
important. By bringing your arm all the way
up, you will get full power out of the blow.
When the uppercut really makes contact with
an opponent, it will be a fierce blow if you
have followed through properly.

To use the right uppercut as a first punch, and not as a follow-up punch, turn slightly right and drop the right side of your body from the shoulder. Then carry on as just described in the last paragraph, although this time you will not have to first set up the uppercut with the left hook. You should finish with your weight, which has gone through the right hand, shifted left, body slightly turned left, and your right heel high with toe touching.

The left uppercut is a lot like a left hook, except the arm is brought upward instead of from the side. Start by dropping your left side. Your arm should be bent and your palm up. Twist right and snap up the left arm, just as with the right uppercut.

Uppercut Drills   Uppercut drills are done in the same way as those for the other punches. The open glove that is the target should be facing palm down and held in the middle of the body. The left glove is the target for the right uppercut, and vice versa.

MORE COMBINATIONS

Now that you have learned several basic punches, you can build a large number of combinations. First off, try the left jab, straight right, and left hook, one after the other. Again, do the combination slowly until you master it. Jab. Then come across with the right, bringing the left back. You are now in position for a left hook, which you should let fly.

Next, start with a left hook and follow with a right uppercut, just as you did when you first practiced the uppercut. Only now practice the combination over and over until you can do it quickly and snappily.

Next, use the hook followed by a straight right. This combination can mean real trouble for your opponent, because it consists of your two power punches.

A more difficult combination starts with the left jab, followed by a left hook and a straight right. Snap out the jab, bring it back, and as you do, drop into position for your hook. Let

Some good combinations:

left jab   to   straight right   to   left hook

left hook   to   right uppercut

left hook   to   straight right

left jab   to   left hook   to   straight right

the hook go and then finish with the right.

To practice combinations in glove drills, your partner must keep moving the target to the proper place for each punch in the series. Therefore, you and he must agree ahead of time which of the combinations to practice.

Combinations are what boxing is really all about. There are few times in a match that you will throw just a single punch. If you score with a punch the chances are it has left your opponent open for another, and in turn still more blows. A boxer who does not take advantage of this fact is throwing away chances to win. A fighter who uses all his weapons can build the greatest number of combinations and thus get the most out of his punches.

There are many more combinations you can use—a double left hook followed by a straight right, for instance—but to really learn combinations, you have to practice them by sparring with another boxer. This is also necessary if you are to learn to defend yourself against an opponent's punches. Knowing how and when to hit is only part of being a good boxer. You also need to escape being struck. There are many ways. When a punch comes in your direction, you can keep it from scoring by simply moving out of the way, by stopping it before it strikes, or pushing it in another direction, so it misses. There is at least one special defense for each kind of punch. Like punches, defensive moves have to be studied and practiced in a real boxing situation. So if you wish to continue boxing beyond this point, it is time to think about joining an organized program. For reasons of safety, when you are ready for actual contact situations, you must be in such a program.

Defense and Tactics

You need to practice defensive maneuvers in an actual contact situation mainly because the only way you can tell you are doing something wrong is when your techniques don't work— and you are hit as a result. Only under such conditions can you develop the timing you need to perfect your defensive skills. The same is true of many other tricks of the boxing ring. To give you an idea of how they work, some of these techniques are briefly decribed here. They are the kinds of moves you will learn in detail as a beginner in an organized program.

DEFENSE

Defense for the Left Jab   The easiest defense against the left jab is called the parry. A parry is a way of knocking a jab off course. A mere flick of the wrist can send even the strongest jab in the wrong direction. To test for yourself if this is true, try the following experiment with your partner.

Have him extend his jab and hold it out as firmly as he can. Take your stance with your nose just an inch away from his out-stretched left glove. With your right arm close to your body and right glove open, quickly flick your right hand at his left glove. Make sure only your forearm moves. Your open hand should briskly slap his glove and knock it to the side, away from and to the left of your head. You will move your part-ner's arm no matter how firmly he tries to hold it.

The parry does not have to be forceful, just sharp and quick. It should not travel more

parrying
a
left jab

slipping a jab

opponent

opponent

than a few inches before striking the jab. Neither should it reach out for the jab. A good boxer holds the parry until the opponent's glove is just a thumb length away from his face before knocking it away. If a boxer reaches out to deflect the jab he exposes his right side to a blow from the opponent.

Slipping the Jab Another way to defend yourself against the jab is to move your head out of the way of the punch using a technique called "slipping." A simple slip is to the outside of the jab. As the jab comes toward you, you shift your weight to your right leg, twisting your body from the waist and toward the right. Your right heel will touch the floor, and your left foot will pivot right. The move will bring your head outside the jab, so that at worst the punch hits your left shoulder. Probably it will miss altogether.

Lever against the Right You probably know that a lever is a tool that provides extra power for moving a heavy object. In boxing, your left arm can be a lever to move a straight right out of the way. As the right comes in range, shoot out your left arm powerfully. Don't aim directly at your opponent, but over his right shoulder, up and slightly to the left. Your left forearm should move inside his right

123

forearm, and the two arms should come into contact. If you use power and lock your elbow at the moment the arms touch, you will send his right outside, making it miss.

Blocking the Left Hook   Your right arm and glove are the best guards against a left hook. If you keep your arm in the position used in the basic stance, it will be there to intercept hooks before they land. The arm will catch hooks on the bicep, forearm, and wrist. Hold it close to the body and move it up, down, or to the side to catch the punch as it comes. Make sure that the arm is bent at the elbow and kept near the right side of your body.

A high left hook to the head, however, will come in above the right arm. Block that punch by quickly raising your right glove to the side of your head. Keep the glove open, with the palm resting on your head and the side of your face. The glove will cushion the blow.

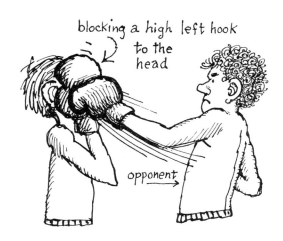

blocking a high left hook to the head

opponent →

Uppercuts Are Easy to Stop You can prevent an uppercut by just shuffling a step or two to the rear. Or if you don't have the shuffle down pat, use a block. To block a left uppercut, cut off the punch by dropping your right

blocking a left uppercut

opponent →

glove, palm open, and catching your opponent at the wrist. Use the left glove in the same way to stop a right uppercut.

Counterpunching When you threw a jab at your partner after parrying his jab, you were doing what boxers call "counterpunching." You were taking advantage of an opening left by your opponent after he threw a punch or made some other kind of move to attack. Some boxers would rather counterpunch than attack first. They wait for their opponent to make the first move, then before he can readjust, they go after him. Whether or not you will box this way is a matter of your own style, but you always should be ready to counterpunch.

Each time you make a correct defensive move against an opponent's blow, you will be in position to counterpunch. For example, when you parry a jab, you are set to throw a left hook, either to the body or head. When

126

you slip a jab to the outside, you are in position to follow up with a straight right, to the jaw or body. After blocking a left hook, counter with one of your own. The leverage block for a straight right sets you up, just like a left jab would, for a return right.

Some boxers will deliberately let a punch hit them if it sets up to deliver a stronger counterpunch. A countering straight right, for instance, can do more damage than a left jab. I once boxed a very tough fighter who was shorter and stronger than I. I kept him at a distance with a left jab, holding him off so he could not reach my body, a better target for him than my head since he was short.

He kept moving in on me, trying for hooks and uppercuts to the body. Each time, I picked him off with a jab or two to the face. It worked fine, until he figured out that since he could not get through my jab, he might as well take it—and then slam me with a hard right.

Look at all the pretty stars !

I jabbed him, and then I saw stars. The moment my jab connected, he whistled a hard right over my extended left hand. He did not spend time trying to block the jab—I was too quick for him—but instead readied himself for a hard right as soon as he saw the jab coming. He hit me several times this way until I realized what he was doing and made sure that when I jabbed I was ready to block the return right. But if he had been just a slightly harder puncher, he might have knocked me out with his right hand before I discovered what he was doing.

TACTICS

If you have been around a boxing gym for even a few weeks, you probably will have heard some boxers described as "ring wise." What this means is that they are very good at planning and using tactics that help them keep the upper hand in the ring, placing their opponents at as much of a disadvantage as possible.

Experienced boxers know dozens of tactics. So will you if you continue very long at the sport. Like defense in boxing, however, tactics are best learned by doing—in the ring—so you should wait to try them until you join an organized program.

For now, however, here is an idea of some very basic tactics and how boxers use them.

Fakes Fakes are moves used to fool an opponent so you can hit him with an unexpected punch. By faking one sort of punch, for instance, you can fool him into guarding against it and leaving himself open for another kind of blow.

You fake by momentarily starting a punch, but never really releasing it. An expert faker can trick his opponent with moves as slight as a twitching shoulder or a slight jerk of the fist. Suppose, for example, you have been scoring on an opponent with your left jab. He may become so worried about your jab that he can think of almost nothing else but defending against it. Bide your time. Then start your jab, but before your fist has moved more than an inch or so, quickly switch to a left hook. If your "act" has been successful, your opponent may try to parry the jab, maybe even reach out, leaving his head and body unguarded.

You also can fake a jab, wait a split second, then throw another jab, this time for real. You

130

may be able to sneak in your jab while your opponent still has his right out of position, trying to parry a punch that wasn't there. Or else, shift your left shoulder slightly forward, fooling your opponent into expecting a left hook. Then come across with your right.

Dropping the left shoulder a bit, or bending just a little at the knees sometimes can make an opponent look out for a body punch. He may drop one or both hands of his guard. That is the time to smack him with a blow to the head, either a straight right or left hook.

Be Smart in the Ring   A good boxer keeps in mind certain rules that help him outwit his opponent. One of the most basic of such tactics is never to try the same move too many times in a row. If you fake a jab and throw a hook time after time, chances are your opponent will soon realize that the fake is a trick. He will be prepared for the hook, blocking it and countering with a strong right.

It is very important never to outpunch your-

Be smart in the ring.

self. Punch only when you have a good chance of hitting the target—and hitting it hard. Do not waste yourself on punches that are out of range or likely to be blocked. If you don't pick and choose your target, you will find yourself punching so often that your arms will tire—you won't have the strength to hold them up—or you'll simply run short of breath.

Another point to remember is never to bend your upper body forward so that your head tilts toward your opponent. All that does is to bring your head—a great target—into your opponent's range. If you happen to have the advantage of height over an opponent, bending toward him can lower your head so much that it will bring you down to his size. I found this out when I was fairly new to boxing. I had been progressing very well and thinking that I was turning into quite a fine boxer after all. Many of my sparring partners, although of the same weight, were of a heavier build and shorter than I. I usually could keep them away with long left jabs. Then one day

I went into the ring with a boxer who was several inches shorter, but very experienced. I found that when I jabbed he moved in low and kept popping me in the stomach. This went on for some time, and all of a sudden, I realized that he was no longer punching my body, but my head. Earlier, although he'd tried, he could not reach my head. What had happened? Had he suddenly grown taller?

No, but in a way I had shrunk, or at least his tactics had made things seem that way. The blows he landed on my midsection weakened the muscles there, and gradually, without knowing it, I'd begun to bend forward at the waist. Eventually, I was so bent over my head was easily in range of his blows.

When fighting someone taller than you, the best tactic is to get in close—by slipping, or perhaps by blocking a punch and moving in—and stay there. This is called infighting. Punch short with straight rights and uppercuts, to the head if you can, or to the body, the best target in that position. Try to keep your forehead close to your opponent, even touching his chest.

By closing with a tall opponent, you prevent him from sticking you repeatedly with punches at long range, where you cannot return the blows. Infighting keeps the tall boxer off balance, and unable to get those long arms of his working at their best.

The tall boxer, on the other hand, should shoot for his short opponent at arm's length, throwing jabs until there is an opening for a power punch. If the short man rushes in—a bad idea for him—just move to the side and punch as he bulls past. In close, keep you arms in the way of his, tying him up until the referee says to "break"—that is, separate and assume the basic stance.

Fighting a Lefty   When a right-hander boxes a lefty, the two fighters often look unskilled. That is because many of the standard methods and tactics do not work as well in this situation, for either boxer. In the first place, the lefty leads with a right. If both fighters jab, the punches will get in each other's way. Neither punch has a good chance of scoring.

The way to get the edge on a lefty is to circle away from his power hand, the left. Always try to position yourself so that his right foot is to the right of your left foot. This may leave you a little open to his right hand, but his left hand will be out of range. What's more, his head and body will be directly in front of your power right.

A left-hander should try to reverse this situation, circling away from the opponent's right hand. The lefty tries to keep his right foot to the left of his opponent's left foot.

At Home in the Ring A master of boxing tactics is a pleasure to watch in the ring. Provided, that is, he has conditioned his body and mind enough to put his tactics into use. Tactics are the last maneuvers a beginner learns.

They come after the boxer discovers how to get into shape, to move, to hit and escape blows. But an understanding of ring tactics helps only if it is built on a base of dedicated training and workouts.

The first steps a new boxer takes are every bit as important as the last. If you plan to enter organized boxing, make sure you learn how to do even the simplest, most basic maneuvers as well as you can. Time spent understanding the proper stance and feeling comfortable with it, for instance, is as important as knowing how to fake an opponent into dropping his guard. Learning one technique at a time with as much accuracy as possible is what will allow you, in the end, to put everything together. When a boxer reaches this stage, the ring becomes his world. He is at home.

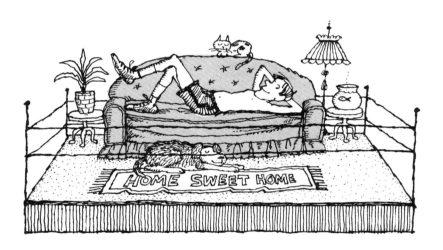

Index

143

About the Author

EDWARD R. RICCIUTI earned degrees from the University of Notre Dame and Columbia University. At Notre Dame he held the university's welterweight championship for two years and in 1957 was named the school's best boxer. A licensed professional second in Connecticut and Massachusetts, he has for many years coached young amateur boxers.

From 1967 to 1972 Mr. Ricciuti was curator of publications and public relations for the New York Zoological Society. A veteran of several scientific expeditions on land and sea and a certified scuba diver, Mr. Ricciuti now devotes full time to writing, lecturing, and television appearances, and serves as consultant to various zoos, aquariums, and conservation organizations. Mr. Ricciuti has written almost twenty books for children and adults. He lives with his family in Killingworth, Connecticut.

About the Illustrator

DON MADDEN, the illustrator of many distinguished books for children, was graduated from the Philadelphia Museum College of Art. His work has been selected for reproduction in the *New York Art Directors' Annual*, in the international advertising art publication *Graphis*, and in the *Society of Illustrators Annual*. He lives with his wife, who is also an artist, and their two children in upstate New York.